Somewhere Between The Earth And The Sky

Raquel S. King

BookLeaf Publishing

Presentation by *BookLeaf Publishing*

Web: www.bookleafpub.com

E-mail: info@bookleafpub.com

ISBN: 9789395969000

First edition 2022

These words are dedicated to the Souls I love who've crossed over to the other side - The ones who look out for me as my Angels and Guides.

And to the people I know who've shared the joy of knowing these Souls - The ones who hold their memories close to their hearts.

ACKNOWLEDGEMENT

Thank you to the friends and family who've supported me along life's journey and to everyone who has encouraged me over the years to work on my creative endeavors.

PREFACE

These writings scrape away at the exterior layers that we regularly exposed to others, and they give permission to wander into a sweet, yet honest vulnerability; a true example of what it means to turn life's proverbial lemons into creative lemonade.

Sometimes

Sometimes
I see myself
In the reflection
Of the city
I breathe in the art
The architecture
The music
And the movement
I momentarily think
'I am a writer -
I belong here!"
And then I remember
I am not fond
Of winter coats

Silver Glow

4.5. and 6 a.m.
A soft silver glow
Seeps through a crack
In a boarded window

A rush of thoughts
Whirls and twirls
Down an endless drain
Water drips
From a broken sink
A cat purrs
A dog snores
A silent spark
In the midst of night

Do the dead say hello
In the form of light?
Does the love we have
Keep them alive?
When the world is sleeping
They exist in my mind

Mosaic Moon

There she was
Smiling in the sky
A devious grin
That came and went
As the clouds passed by

Time slowed down
The rain began
Tiny droplets
Playfully danced
During a windy serenade

The colorless moon
Now fragmented light
A rainbow of tears
Reminding the world
Of the beautifully broken

Heavy Hearts

People sit
In quite houses
With idol hands
Heavy hearts
And loud minds

Senseless distractions
Staring, scrolling
Emissions of blue light
Penetrate sad eyes

We could be painting
Soul chasing
Star gazing
But instead, we stare
Into tiny blue screens

Yearning for more
Longing for meaning

The Word 'Was'

A small circular window
Endless white skies
And a muted orange
Faintly apparent
Far below

On an isolated seat
In the back of a plane
There is a girl
Quietly contemplating
An emotional read

At the bottom
Of page 48

She takes in the name
Of A lifeless child

Lily
Yes, This was her name
The word 'was'
Loud and clear

The period
At the end

Of a sad, sad sentence
Quickly became
A Silent tear

The girl on the plane
Thought some more
About all of the people
Whose names associate
With the sad word 'was'

In between
The tiny cracks
Of her broken heart
She held some space
For the people who 'were'
Especially the ones
Whose names
Are Lily

Maybe So

Somewhere in between
The maybe this
Or maybe that
I find a strange
Sense of comfort
For it is the certainties of life
Or the certainties of death rather
That burden me with sadness

Because somewhere
Within the 'maybe'
There are things
And people
And outcomes
That still exist

Ever Changing

The clouds
They move
They change

They do not know
That they are clouds
They just are
Simply clouds

Existing in their
Ever-changing beauty
Like the clouds
We will continue to change
A simple truth we must
Soberly embrace

This is our blessing
This is our curse
This is what it means
To be perfectly human

Spontaneous Dance

Sounds of music
A spontaneous dance
Awkward tension
Turns to grounding movements
A slow release
With a bend in the knees
And a dangle of hands

A celtic voice
Fills the room
With feminine energy
And food for the soul
Be in this body
Love this vessel
For it is a gift

A fire burns
Deep in the belly
With tribal nature
And fluid motion
Feet Stop
Arms flare
Voices echo
Bodies vibrate

Clear stagnation
Feel liberation
Finally find
The freedom within

Galaxy Of Stars

The epitome of youth
With an old soul spirit
His eyes twinkled
Like a galaxy of stars
Full of effervescent light

Now that he's no longer
here on this earth
I often wonder
If what they say
Is it true

Are the stars really
Holes in the sky
Where lost love shines?
And I often think
I still see his light

When I look at the sky
I see my brother
It's because of him
That wherever we go
We go with all our heart

Pink Fluffy Clouds

Her soul allowed others
To feel safe and accepted
To take off their masks
And be their true selves

Her laugh was as warm
As a summer afternoon
Her hugs all encompassing
Like a pink fluffy cloud

The day she left
This earthly plane
We thought we'd never
See a rainbow again

Yet her sparkle blazed on
And with each fiery sunset
We're reminded that
Her light is still here

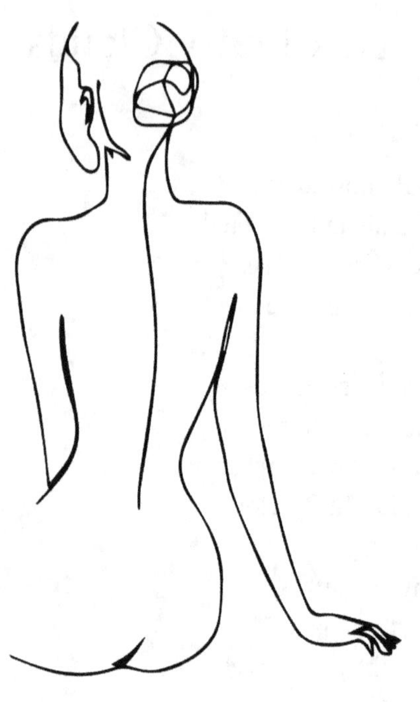

Vastness of Space

I somehow came to believe
That the nonexistence of true love
Was more fathomable
Then the notion of love at first sight

And then we met

I hoped that night
Would never end
But the sun came up
As it tends to do

As fate would have it
Our lives interlaced
A cosmic love
As vast as space

Then came the day
That we parted ways
Yet sometimes we'd meet
In the land of dreams

Your earthly departure
Taught me to believe
In the the unwavering notion
Of a timeless love

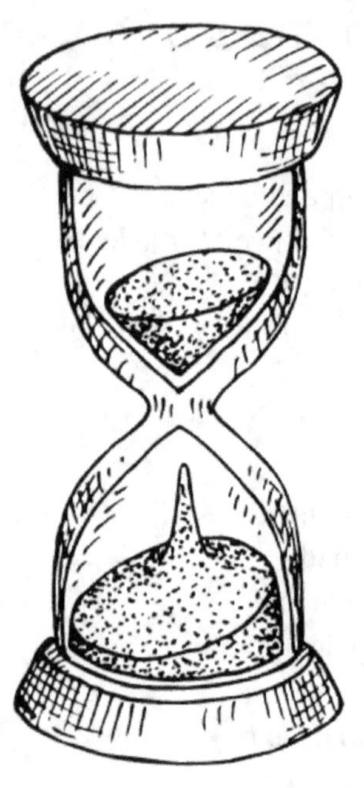

Sapphire Ocean

Magic beamed
From his sapphire eyes
His laugh, more intoxicating
Then the cocktails
We were drinking

He needed care
I needed affection
Together we tended
To our incurable maladies

He taught me that true love
Can happen more than once
But only if you're lucky
Only if you let it

The day he departed
I prayed to a God
Whom I wasn't sure existed
To help me understand
Why love alone can't save us

When I look at the ocean
I can still see his eyes

When I hear the waves break
I feel my heart
Go back with the tide
To the place I know
We will one day return

A Beating Heart

Other kids made decisions
About where to go to college
While I made decisions
About another being's future

Would I have the strength
To do this myself
Or would it be better
To give you a life
With someone else?

My confidence grew
With the intensity of
Your beating heart

I would find a way
As mothers often do
To give you a life
Of meaning and love

But your beating heart
One day stopped
And you never took
That first sweet breath

While other kids
Carried books to school
I carried the weight
Of life and death

Although you were small
Your impact was immense
It was from you that I learned
Love does not die

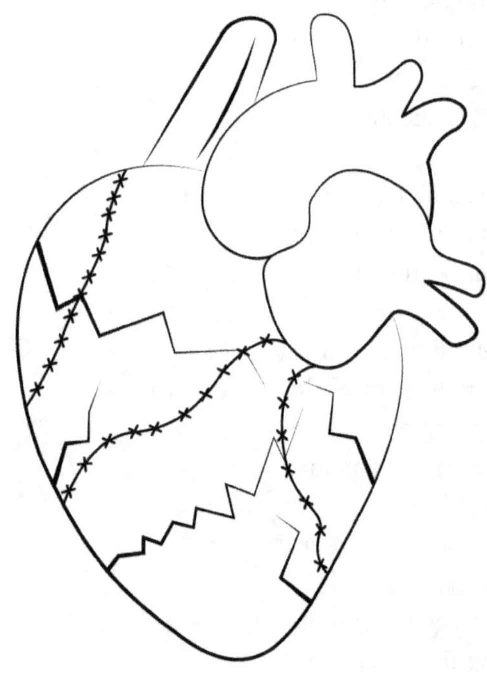

Through The Door

The train disappeared
Like a distant memory
As I stepped into
The brick laid house

Carefully closing
The door behind me

The floors creaked
And moonlight seeped
Through a bedroom window

There I lay
In tangled sheets

The morning sun
Had yet to rise
The world was motionless
In its silent slumber

Leaving Nashville

The plane ascends
I press my face
Against the glass
While gazing upon
A breathtaking sunset

The moving clouds
Begin to resemble
A mountain like city

Touched by the paintbrush
Of Salvador Dali

The clouds play along
With the golden sun
A swirl of purple wisps
Waltz above
Warm tangerine
Spread throughout the sky

For an instant
I see a your face
In the wispy clouds

Slowly it dissipates
As the sun melts
Beyond the horizon

South Beach

The Sky
A quiet opal blue

Tiny puffs
Of dark gray clouds
Hover above
A sea-foam colored ocean

The clouds stand still
Despite the elegant breeze

In the distance
Silhouettes dance
To Balkan beats

A girl wanders off
Her sandy blond hair
Blows wildly in the wind

Her dress flows freely
As she dreamily sashays
Towards a handsome young man

He spins her around
In a moment of bliss

Stealing a long
Sensual kiss

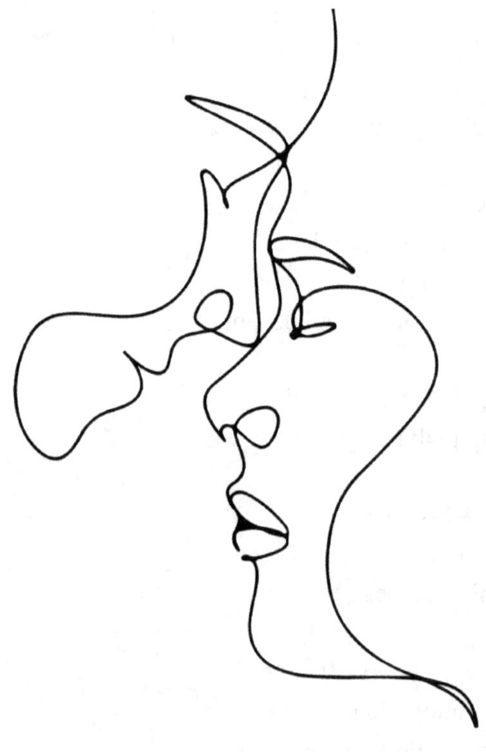

New Orleans

I know of a place
Where magic seems real
And time does not

Where houses
And streets
And tiny objects
Have a life of their own

A place where books
Bewitchingly appear
Directly in one's path

Here in this place
Cemeteries have souls
And souls have music

That blare from horns
And sing from strings

Somehow here
In this mystical place
Paintings perfectly depict
The visual of sound

And the voices
Of past lives
Echo softly
Along the edge
Of the Mississippi river

Cherry Blossoms

A waning moon,
In all her ephemeral glory
Rested gently
In an amethyst sky

Her colors changed
From pale pink
To a soft and subtle gold

She moved slowly
In her far away dance
Yet she remained so opulent

That I could still see
Lingering leaves on the trees

As the moonlight beamed
The petals bloomed
Blushing with variations
Of peach and rose
And pearly white

I stretched my arms out
Up towards the trees
Which swayed ever so slightly

Beyond my reach
I longed to hold
The fleeting beauty
Of their fallen petals
In the cusps of my hands

And whisper
'Thank You'